Y0-BBF-051

Witness History Series

THE WAR IN VIETNAM

Michael Gibson

The Bookwright Press
New York · 1992

Titles in this series

The Arab-Israeli Conflict
Blitzkrieg!
China since 1945
The Cold War
The Origins of World War I
The Origins of World War II
The Rise of Fascism
The Russian Revolution

South Africa since 1948
The Third Reich
The United Nations
The United States since 1945
The USSR under Stalin
War in the Trenches
The War in Vietnam

Cover illustration: A North Vietnamese propaganda poster proclaiming the "destruction of U.S. military power by the elusive guerrillas."

First published in the
United States in 1992 by
The Bookwright Press
387 Park Avenue South
New York, NY 10016

First published in 1991 by
Wayland (Publishers) Ltd
61 Western Road, Hove
East Sussex BN3 1JD
England

© Copyright 1991 Wayland (Publishers) Ltd

Library of Congress Cataloging-in-Publication Data
Gibson, Michael, 1936-
 War in Vietnam / Michael Gibson.
  p. cm. — (Witness history)
 Includes bibliographical references and index.
 Summary: Examines the origins and outcome of the civil war in Vietnam, discussing the roles played by France, the United States, the Soviet Union, and other nations and parties involved in the conflict.
  ISBN 0-531-18408-0
  1. Vietnamese Conflict, 1961-1975 — Juvenile literature.
 [1. Vietnamese Conflict, 1961-1975.] I. Title. II. Series: Witness history series.
 DS557.7.G534 1992
 959.704'3—dc20   91-9134
                                          CIP
                                           AC

Typeset by Kalligraphic Design Limited, Horley, Surrey
Printed by G. Canale & C.S.p.A., Turin, Italy

Contents

'Nam 4

1 A history of struggle 1887–1954
Vietnam: the country 6
Ho Chi Minh 8
War with France 10
The French withdraw 12

2 The U.S. moves in 1954–68
Civil war 14
Flaming Dart and Rolling Thunder 16
Search and destroy 18
Tet 20

3 A guerrilla war
Guerrilla warfare 22
A soldier's lot . . . 24
Hunters and killers 26
The electronic battlefield 28

4 Terror and atrocities
War crimes 30
Chemical warfare 32
South Vietnam at war 34
North Vietnam at war 36

5 A hard road to peace 1968–73
Nixon's war 38
"Hell no, we won't go!" 40
Red flag over Saigon 42

6 The legacy of Vietnam
A poor country 44
Censorship and war 46
How was a superpower beaten? 48
Lessons learned? 50

Leading figures 52

Important dates 56

Glossary 58

Further reading 60

Notes on sources 61

Index 62

'NAM

THE VIETNAM WAR was not the longest or bloodiest war in history, but it epitomized the struggle between the superpowers, the United States and the Soviet Union.

From 1861 to 1940, Vietnam was part of France's Far Eastern empire. During World War II, the Japanese (the Nazis' Pacific allies) shared power in Vietnam with the French. Vietnamese nationalists of all political persuasions resisted the Japanese, hoping to obtain independence for their country. But after the war, the French tried to regain their colony. The nationalists rose up against them; this was the first phase of the Vietnam War.

By 1954, when the French were forced to withdraw, Vietnam north of the seventeenth parallel was dominated by Ho Chi Minh's communists, and to the south by an American-backed regime. Attempts to coexist did not last, and civil war broke out between the North – supported by the Soviet Union – and the South, aided by the United States. Northern military successes eventually brought the Americans into the war to support the South. This phase of the war lasted from 1964 to 1973. Although the United States withdrew in 1973 and Vietnam was unified two years later, conflict continued in Vietnam's neighboring countries, Cambodia and Laos.

Between 1945 and 1973 the war cost at least two million Vietnamese, seventy-four thousand French and fifty-eight thousand American lives. The economic costs of the war were incalculable. The United States may have spent $120 billion between 1965 and 1973.

Heavily armed and equipped American troops cross a river passing through tropical forest. Little attempt has been made to camouflage the soldiers.

The following account gives some idea of what the war was like for an ordinary American soldier in 1968. On reaching Saigon, an officer told him:

> This is the program for the day: You're going to get killed in Vietnam. We're in our own world here. If you don't do what I tell you, you're going to be taken out of our world. [1]

The old rules were gone, and life was cheap and dangerous here.

During the Tet Offensive (see page 20), this soldier was guarding the perimeter of Long Binh camp:

> There were Gooks [North Vietnamese] on the wire that night . . . We shot a few of them. I killed a couple myself. I thought in the back of my mind that I was going to break down and cry because I killed one, but to me it was nothing . . . [2]

North Vietnamese soldiers line up for inspection in front of their tanks in 1969. This heavy armor would have been imported from either the Soviet Union or China.

The Vietnamese communists were formidable opponents:

> The VC [Vietcong] came with a human-wave attack. They wore black pajamas or just regular clothes. But they had all kinds of Chinese and Russian weapons – flamethrowers, rocket launchers etc. [3]

The North Vietnamese soldier "held his ground. He was well indoctrinated, he knew what his mission was." [4]

In the Vietnam War, a small country defeated a major superpower. The communists took over the whole of Vietnam. An American military expert Colonel Summers told a North Vietnamese colonel after the war, "You know, you never defeated us on the battlefield." To which his communist counterpart replied, "That may be so, but it is also irrelevant." [5]

1
A HISTORY OF STRUGGLE: 1887–1954
Vietnam: the country

During the second half of the nineteenth century, the French came to regard Indochina as their sphere of influence. In 1887 they created the Indochinese Union, composed of Cochin-China, Annam, Tonkin and Cambodia; Laos was added to the Union six years later.

The French did not establish their authority easily. The Vietnamese fought back using guerrilla tactics. A French commander commented sorrowfully:

> *We have had enormous difficulties in enforcing our authority... Rebel bands disturb the country everywhere. They appear from nowhere in large numbers, destroy everything and disappear into nowhere.* [6]

These rebels were subjected to great brutality by the French, who destroyed whole villages accused of hiding guerrillas. The French tried to impose their lifestyle, ideas, educational system and culture upon the Vietnamese. But the Vietnamese already had a very ancient and sophisticated culture, which most Vietnamese people thought was superior to that of the French invaders.

The colonial government fully exploited Vietnam economically. Paul Doumer, who was the governor-general of Indochina from 1897, stated that "when France arrived in Indochina, the Annamites were ripe for servitude." [7] This statement shows France's imperialist attitude toward the Vietnamese.

Before the French arrived, most Vietnamese peasants had owned their own

The French enlisted the people of Indochina in their colonial forces: this picture shows the Vietnamese soldiers from Tonkin in 1888.

A history of struggle 1887–1954

This is a map of Indochina in the 1930s. Cochin-China, Annam and Tonkin are parts of Vietnam. Cambodia and Laos are the other countries in Indochina. Most of the coastal area is covered with tropical forest with monsoon forest farther inland.

land. French colonists took control of a large area of territory, and, by the 1930s, 70 percent of Vietnam's peasants were poor, landless tenants. The French developed mines and rubber plantations, but they kept wages low, arguing that their profits depended upon cheap labor. The glaring difference between the luxurious way of life of most French colonists and the poverty of the Vietnamese laborers created huge resentment.

Some French politicians realized that reforms were needed if they were to maintain control in Vietnam, but little was done. France officially recognized Bao Dai as the Emperor of Vietnam in 1932, but real power lay with some five thousand French officials. Vietnamese nationalists started to demand self-government, but without success. Frustration led to violence, and from time to time leading colonists were murdered or their property was attacked. The situation became increasingly dangerous.

The Vietnamese became increasingly determined to rid themselves of French colonial rule.

Ho Chi Minh

An extract from the Indochinese Communist Party's Manifesto in 1930:

1. *To overthrow imperialism, the feudal system and the reactionary bourgeoisie in Vietnam.*
2. *To win complete independence for Indochina.*
3. *To form a government made up of workers, peasants and soldiers.*
4. *To nationalize the banks . . . and place them under the control of the proletarian [people's] government.*
5. *To confiscate the agricultural estates owned by the imperialists [French] and bourgeois reactionaries [the ruling class] in order to share them out among the poor peasants.*
6. *To introduce the eight-hour working day.*
7. *To abolish compulsory loans, the poll tax and other abusive laws.*
8. *To give the people democratic liberties.*
9. *To provide education for all.*
10. *To achieve sexual equality.* [8]

Among the Vietnamese population, the upper and middle classes were to take a backseat according to the communist program.

Ho Chi Minh, one of the most influential figures in world communism, was born in 1890 in a village in central Vietnam. His father,

In this picture, Ho Chi Minh is presented in a romantic light, dressed in a simple uniform.

A history of struggle 1887–1954

A scene from the Russian Revolution of 1917, which led to the formation of the first communist state in the world. Lenin is speaking, and behind him stand Stalin and Trotsky.

a mandarin, abandoned his career, his wife and children and roamed the country as a medicine man. After a difficult childhood, Ho signed on as a stoker aboard a French freighter in 1911 and spent three years traveling around the world before settling in Paris.

In Paris, he helped to found the French Communist Party, and in 1924 he moved to Moscow where he met Trotsky and Stalin, the leaders of Soviet communism. As a communist organizer, he established the Indochinese Communist Party in 1930. Like all nationalists, Ho wanted to obtain complete freedom for his country from colonial rule. Like many reformers, he wanted to make Vietnam a democracy, to provide education for all, to introduce a shorter working day and to abolish unfair taxes.

Many years later, Ho explained that "it was patriotism and not communism that originally inspired me." [9] But he was impressed by the communist revolution in the Soviet Union. It seemed at that time that the Soviet Union had the potential power to spark a world communist revolution that would liberate Vietnam and all the other countries suffering under the yoke of a foreign power.

In 1940 the Japanese occupied Vietnam, but left the French administration intact. Shortly afterward, Ho returned to his country, after thirty years abroad. He realized that he could not carry out a communist revolution with his small band of followers. So he set about organizing resistance groups, called the Vietminh, which united "all patriots without distinction of wealth, age, sex, religion or political outlook." [10]

When Japan was defeated, at the end of World War II, Ho hoped that the Vietnamese working classes would be strong enough to carry out a communist revolution. But French forces, with British assistance, reoccupied the country very quickly. Incidentally, at this time the United States favored independence for Vietnam.

Ho had to be content with setting up a nationalist government in North Vietnam. He was prepared to cooperate with other parties until such a time as the communists were strong enough to establish their own regime. Although Ho did not approve of the way the Soviet Union dominated world communism, he was prepared to make use of Soviet aid to win independence for his beloved country.

War with France

No sooner was World War II over than the Vietnamese Emperor, Bao Dai, resigned and Ho announced the creation of a Democratic Republic. He hoped for American support, since he had cooperated with the Allies during World War II.

Ho's declaration, however, upset the plan concocted by the Allies at the Potsdam Peace Conference in July 1945 to disarm the Japanese in Vietnam by dividing the country at the sixteenth parallel. The British were to control the South, the Chinese the North. There was no mention in the plan of independence for Vietnam.

The British commander in Vietnam, General Gracey, was unable to control South Vietnam, so in September 1945 he released the French army troops who had been interned by the Japanese. Battles between the French and the Vietnamese ensued.

Meanwhile, in the North, Ho Chi Minh established a nationalist government that included non-communists and began to implement limited, rather than revolutionary, reforms. He abolished heavy taxes and made prostitution, opium smoking, gambling and the sale of alcohol illegal. In spite of his pleas for moderation, some landlords were stripped of their estates and punished by local "people's courts."

In September 1945 the Chinese soldiers delegated to disarm the Japanese arrived in Vietnam. Ho was now trapped. The Chinese were attempting to take control in the North; the French in the South. The Soviet Union had not offered support, and the United States had

The Emperor Bao Dai of Vietnam is shown with President Auriol of France in 1953, discussing the possibility of granting Vietnam independence within the French Union.

A history of struggle 1887–1954

This gun was used during the war with France. The North Vietnamese built this museum in 1984 to record their victory over the French.

indicated that it would back France. Ho was under pressure to compromise.

In March 1946 France recognized Vietnam as a free state within the French Union (the new French commonwealth). The nature of the government in Cochin-China, in the South, was to be decided by a referendum. But in May the French commander, D'Argenlieu, proclaimed a Republic of Cochin-China in the name of the French government.

The French were determined to take over the North too, and in November 1946, French warships shelled Haiphong, killing six thousand people, while French troops moved north. Ho and his lieutenant General Giap organized guerrilla forces to resist their advance.

A French officer wrote:

> *If we departed believing a region pacified, the Vietminh would arrive on our heels . . . There was only one possible defense, to multiply our posts, fortify them and train the villagers, coordinate intelligence and the police.* [11]

"Pacifying" the region, of course, meant subduing it under French control.

After World War II the Soviet Union established communist regimes in the eastern European countries, and in 1949 a communist government was proclaimed in China. Shortly afterward, on January 14, 1950, Ho created the Democratic Republic of Vietnam in the North. The French retaliated by setting up "the Republic of Vietnam within the French Union" in the South. Vietnam became two warring states, divided roughly along the seventeenth parallel.

The United States was determined to prevent the further spread of communism. When communist North Koreans invaded South Korea in June 1950, President Truman sent American troops to support the South. He also granted the French $15 million to finance their war in Indochina.

The French withdraw

In 1950 the communist state of China, followed by the Soviet Union, recognized the Democratic Republic of Vietnam. The Vietminh accepted gifts of Chinese automatic weapons, mortars, howitzers and trucks. With their help, General Giap created a regular army capable of defeating the French in the field.

By late 1952 the French had suffered more than ninety thousand dead, wounded and captured. But the French government stubbornly refused to accept the verdict of General Navarre, the commander in Indochina, that "there was no possibility of winning the war."[12] They had to evacuate North Vietnam and a good part of Laos.

These evacuees leaving North Vietnam in August 1954 are being checked by the French authorities before moving to centers in the South. Many of the refugees were Catholics, fearful of the new communist government.

Communist troops advancing to take Haiphong, one of the most important ports in North Vietnam.

During 1953 Vietminh forces assembled to attack Dien Bien Phu, the last great French stronghold. In March 1954 General Giap began the offensive. He admitted that his forces suffered terrible casualties, but reported that "our fighters dug hundreds of kilometers of trenches. Now, we can move in open country despite enemy napalm and artillery." [13]

The possibility of a French defeat alarmed the United States. Some of President Eisenhower's advisers suggested he use atomic weapons to destroy the Vietminh, but the president refused. Such a move could have involved other world powers and could possibly have led to a third world war. The Vietminh defeated the French at Dien Bien Phu; they were now in control of more than three-quarters of Vietnam. The communist red flag was hoisted over the French command bunker on May 7, 1954. The shock of defeat forced France to the negotiating table. At the Geneva Conference a ceasefire was arranged. North and South Vietnam were to be divided along the seventeenth parallel until country-wide elections in 1956. The Vietminh had to give up the areas they held in the South.

Why did the French lose the war?
- Initially, the French enjoyed great armament advantage, but gradually the Vietminh, with Chinese help, achieved roughly the same level of equipment.
- The French did not achieve sufficient mobility to move their troops rapidly to wherever they were needed.
- The French troops were heavily outnumbered by the Vietminh who were secretly supported by many ordinary Vietnamese. General Navarre summed up the reasons for Vietminh success:

Our adversaries were fighting a complete war in which all disciplines – politics, the economy, propaganda – were involved. [14]

In contrast to the Vietnamese, who were fighting for their own land, the French never threw themselves wholeheartedly into the war. As early as 1947, an opinion poll had shown that 36 percent of French people questioned supported the war, 42 percent favored a negotiated peace and 8 percent thought the French should withdraw from Indochina. [15]

2
THE U.S. MOVES IN: 1954–68
Civil war

THE OFFICIAL ENDING of the Indochinese war in 1954 brought little relief. The South Vietnamese regime led by Ngo Dinh Diem (1954–63) was inefficient and corrupt. Diem refused to hold free elections because "people in the villages admired Ho Chi Minh as they thought he stood for an independent Vietnam, free from the colonial yoke." [16] He was afraid that Ho would win the elections.

Although Diem attempted some land reform, his regime raised rents for the peasants and took away their control of local affairs. By contrast, Ho stripped the North Vietnamese landowners of their estates, a process many resisted and cost fifty thousand lives.

By 1958 an opposition movement was growing in South Vietnam. The National Front for the Liberation of Vietnam (NLF) called for the overthrow of the Diem government in favor of a "broad national coalition."

The NLF was nicknamed "Vietcong" by the government, which stood for "Vietnamese communists."

In a major effort to defeat the Vietcong, Diem launched the Strategic Hamlet program. In the areas where guerrillas were active, villagers were taken away from their homes and relocated in fortified camps. But many people continued to collaborate with the Vietcong, because it opposed the corrupt government and demanded change. Others cooperated with the Vietcong because they were intimidated by them into doing so.

In 1959 the North Vietnamese started smuggling advisers and weapons down the "Ho Chi Minh Trail" through neutral Cambodia and Laos into South Vietnam. Diem tried to stop South Vietnamese villagers from helping the Vietcong by imprisoning large numbers of suspected sympathizers.

President Ngo Dinh Diem with his family in Saigon. The lifestyle of the ruling Vietnamese was rich and luxurious.

The U.S. moves in 1954–68

THE DOMINO THEORY

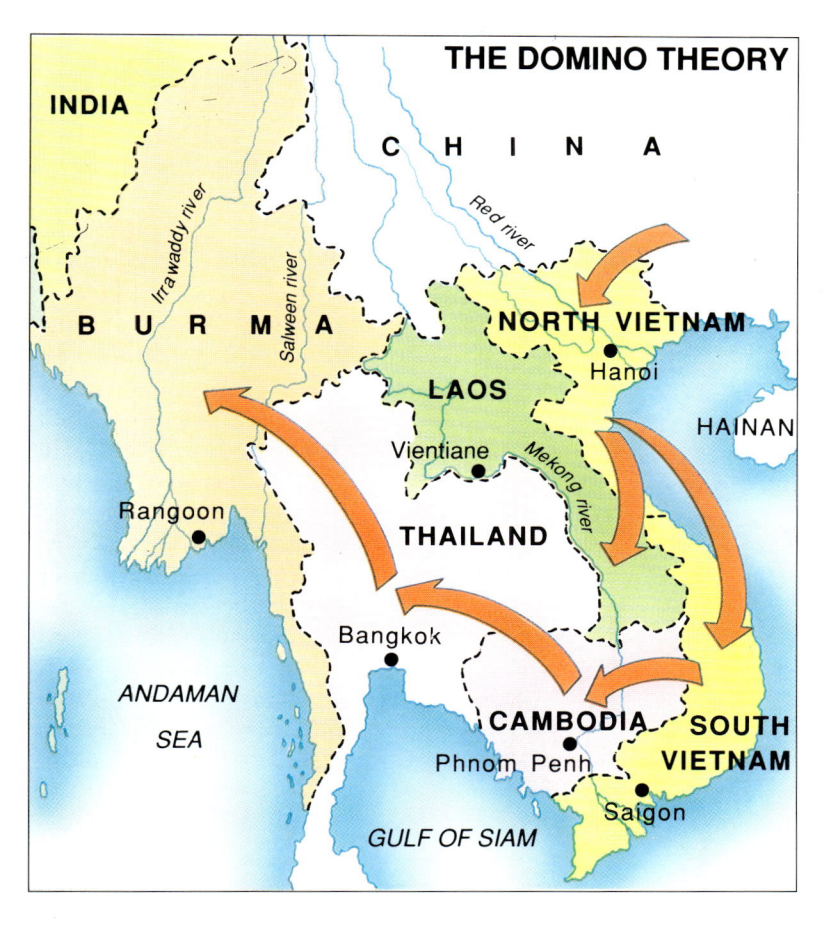

▲ A Dallas newspaper report from the day after John F. Kennedy's assassination.

◀ The arrows show how communism might have spread, according to the Domino Theory.

When North Vietnam introduced universal military conscription in April 1960, the United States seriously considered sending troops to South Vietnam. When, later in the year, the Vietminh joined with the Vietcong to form the National Liberation Front for South Vietnam, the United States propped up Diem's regime with more aid.

Fighting had broken out in Laos between the Royal Lao army and the communist Pathet Lao in 1959. In January 1962 President Eisenhower warned his successor, John Kennedy, that he faced a major crisis:

If we let South Vietnam fall [to the communists], the next domino Laos, Cambodia, Burma and on down into the Subcontinent will fall. [17]

This was the Domino Theory, which Kennedy took very seriously. It was events in Laos that worried him so much. As President Diem's popularity continued to dwindle, Kennedy decided to send in more American advisers "to help South Vietnam resist communist pressures." The number of these advisers, first sent out in 1961, was increased to ten thousand in 1962 and fourteen thousand in 1963.

By mid-1963 it became clear that the well-equipped South Vietnamese army of two hundred thousand could not contain the Vietcong guerrillas in the Mekong delta. President Kennedy openly criticized Diem on television. Shortly afterward, on November 2, South Vietnamese army officers staged a coup, murdering Diem in the process. On November 22 Kennedy was assassinated and replaced by Lyndon Johnson.

15

Flaming Dart and Rolling Thunder

The new president of the United States, Lyndon Johnson, vowed:

> I am not going to lose Vietnam. I am not going to be the president who saw southeast Asia go the way China went. [18]

China was now a communist nation, and Johnson perceived the United States as the principal bulwark against further spread of communism.

The Vietcong, however, seemed close to taking control of South Vietnam. American strategists devised a plan to wipe out the North Vietnamese forces from the air and awaited a pretext to carry it out.

On August 2, 1964, it was reported that North Vietnamese patrol boats attacked the USNS *Maddox*, a U.S. destroyer, in the Gulf of Tonkin. Two days later, another destroyer, which had been sent to assist the *Maddox*, also reported it was under attack. After the war, considerable doubt was raised as to whether these attacks had actually happened. In any case, President Johnson announced:

> Renewed hostile actions against United States ships on the high seas have today required me to order the military forces of the United States to take action in reply. [19]

Sixty-four naval aircraft attacked North Vietnam and within ten minutes destroyed 10 percent of its oil supplies. To many, this reaction seemed more offensive than defensive.

Once again, international developments heightened tension. In October 1964 China exploded its first atomic bomb, and the new leaders of the Soviet Union showed little inclination toward peaceful coexistence with the West. In American ruling circles the Vietnam crisis was discussed: should the United States intervene militarily, or should it accept the risk of a communist takeover in South Vietnam, further increasing communist influence in the region? Meanwhile, during 1964 the Vietcong doubled its forces to 170,000.

Vietcong attacks upon U.S. installations in Vietnam provoked Johnson into authorizing Operation Flaming Dart in February 1965.

This quotation from Lyndon Johnson's speech in January 1964 is used here by a satirical cartoonist in the British newspaper, the *Evening Standard*, December 1965.

"LET THIS SESSION OF CONGRESS BE KNOWN AS THE SESSION — WHICH DECLARED ALL-OUT WAR ON HUMAN POVERTY"

The U.S. moves in 1954–68

Forty-nine A-4 Skyhawks and F-8 Crusaders attacked the Dong Hoi barracks. In March, Operation Rolling Thunder was initiated: within minutes, bridges, railroad lines and port facilities had been obliterated by intensive bombing. President Johnson claimed, "We have carefully limited the raids . . . They have been directed at concrete and steel not at human life." [20] However, the bombing of such facilities could not avoid causing civilian casualties. A week later the first U.S. combat troops landed in Vietnam.

American involvement in the war escalated at a frightening speed. The bombing raids were stepped up and American troop levels were raised from 23,300 at the end of 1964 to 184,300 at the end of 1965.

Why, in a matter of a few weeks, had President Johnson moved from a policy of neutrality to outright war? Later, Johnson admitted that his decision was largely political. He wanted to ensure that his party, the Democrats, could win the next election and pass reforms to alleviate poverty and create "the Great Society." He believed that defeat in Vietnam would lead to a Republican victory.

◀ The Americans prepare to retaliate after the Vietcong attack on Bien Hoa, November 1965. The phrase "Sorry about that," written on the shell, became a famous saying among U.S. soldiers.

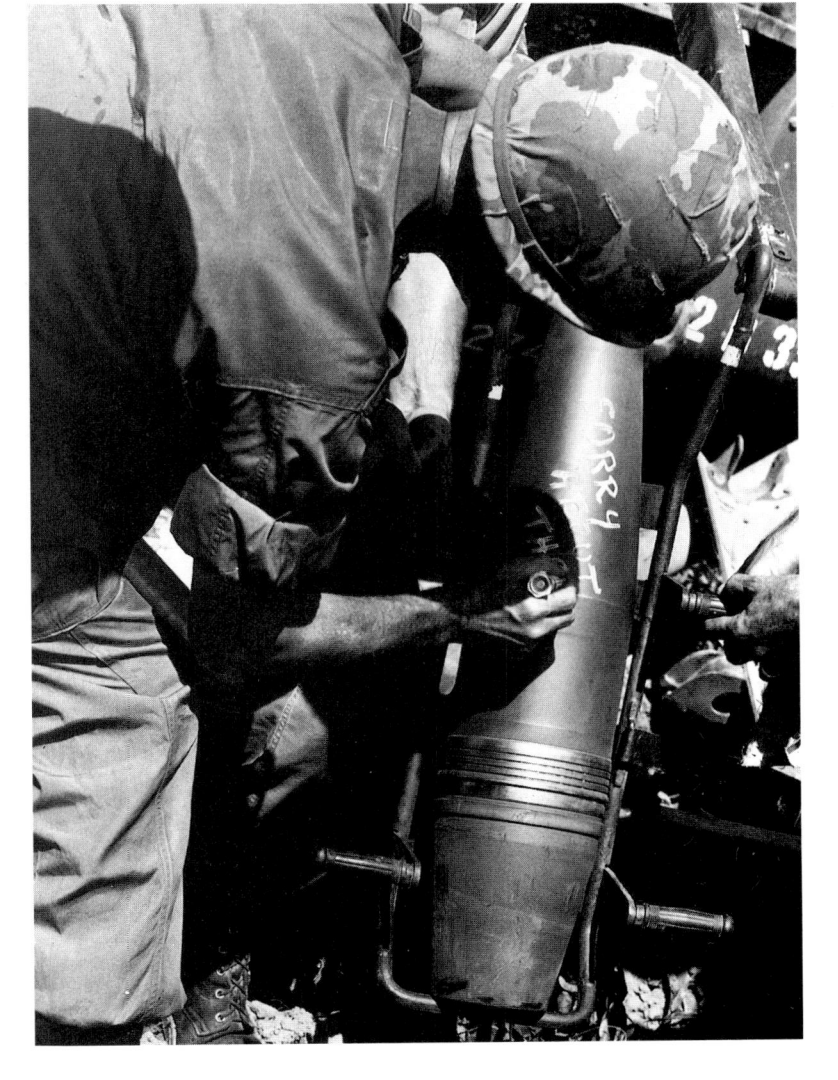

▼ Pictures such as this one, showing cheerful North Vietnamese leaving their village to fight the Americans, were used by the Vietnam News Agency in Hanoi as part of the propaganda war.

Search and destroy

Early in 1965 the United States used the "carrot and stick" method of negotiation with Ho Chi Minh. The "carrot" of economic aid was offered in return for peace, and if the communists did not accept, the "stick" – increased American military intervention – was used. The North Vietnamese rejected the offer of aid with scorn.

In May and June 1965 the Vietcong destroyed five South Vietnamese combat regiments and nine battalions. The government collapsed, and General Nguyen Van Thieu became the new head of state. The United States poured in more troops to help Thieu, including forces from allied countries, such as Australia. The bombing of North Vietnam continued, and in October the Americans defeated the North Vietnamese in the first conventional battle of the war in the Iadrang Valley. More U.S. victories followed.

Success led to confidence. General William Westmoreland, the U.S. commander, predicted that the war would be over by the end of 1967. In contrast, a CIA study concluded that even a big American force would fail to halt the communists. In 1966, the allies carried out their first "Search and Destroy" mission in Binh Dinh province. Large numbers of troops swept the area killing suspected communists: the "body count" was 2,389 dead. In addition, fighter-bombers dropped 1.5 million pounds of bombs on North Vietnam.

This picture, entitled "Carrying the Enemy," shows two U.S. soldiers leading away a Vietcong guerrilla they have captured from the bunker in the background, January 1966.

The U.S. moves in 1954–68

The Ho Chi Minh Trail.

Yet a woman Vietcong soldier commented:

> *The Americans thought that the more bombs they dropped, the quicker we would fall to our knees and surrender. But the bombs heightened rather than dampened our spirit.* [21]

The guerrilla forces multiplied, and they were supported by the Soviet Union and China. Munitions and reinforcements were smuggled along the Ho Chi Minh Trail through Cambodia and Laos to South Vietnam. By mid-1967 U.S. forces had reached 431,000 and there was no sign of the war ending.

Westmoreland's prediction had proved to be incorrect. The U.S. strategy had failed. Search and Destroy missions had proved expensive: American combat casualties rose from 6,644 in 1966 to over 16,000 in 1967. Westmoreland had tried to starve the Vietcong into submission by driving the peasants into the towns. But once the troops had passed by, the communists slipped back into the cleared areas and took control. The policy of "forced urbanization" merely reinforced support for the Vietcong among the South Vietnamese people.

Having held the Americans and their allies in check, the communists planned to annihilate the South Vietnamese army and force the United States to withdraw, by fighting a decisive battle in South Vietnam. The New Year (called Tet in Vietnamese) of 1968 was to be the setting for this knockout blow.

Tet

On January 31, 1968, the Vietnamese New Year, the communists launched surprise attacks on every major South Vietnamese town and city. "Our main objective was to inspire uprisings throughout the South," wrote a leading communist.[22] At the time, the area was occupied by a million American and South Vietnamese soldiers!

The fighting was ferocious. At Hue on February 25, the Americans found the mass graves of people killed by the Vietcong. An eyewitness recorded:

> We saw corpses of Vietnamese civilians who had been buried alive, faces frozen in mid-scream, hands like claws, the fingernails bloody and caked with damp earth.[23]

The Vietcong killed about three thousand people, many of whom were unconnected with the South Vietnamese regime. Although the Vietcong withdrew from Hue and many other cities, the battle for Khesanh raged on for seventy-seven days. At first, the North Vietnamese gained the initiative, but the Americans retaliated by launching the most concentrated air attack the world had witnessed.

By March the main Vietcong offensive had been defeated: the Americans had lost two thousand soldiers, the South Vietnamese four thousand and the North Vietnamese forty thousand. And yet it was not clear who had won! Compare the following opinions to assess the gains and losses of each side:

- Robert McNamara, the U.S. defense secretary, concluded that "the bombing was valueless, it risked the lives of our men (air crew), it killed civilians, and it was not

This South Vietnamese police chief killed a guerrilla in front of TV cameras.

The U.S. moves in 1954–68

Reds shelling Saigon!
8 other cities hit in biggest drive of war

preventing the North Vietnamese from moving to the battle area." [24]

- The broadcasting of the horrifying battles of the Tet Offensive on television networks around the world had a significant effect on public opinion, especially in the United States. In a survey after the Khesanh siege, one in five Americans were found to be against the war, and many expressed the feeling that the United States should win or simply get out of Vietnam.
- As a consequence President Johnson decided not to run again for the presidency.
- Dr. Duong Quynh Hoa, a leading communist, admitted, "We lost our best people." [25]
- Tran Do, a North Vietnamese, observed:

The Tet Offensive hits the headlines in Chicago, January 30, 1968. In spite of warnings, the United States was caught by surprise.

We didn't achieve our main objective, which was to spur uprisings throughout the South . . . As for making an impact on the United States, it had not been our intention – but it turned out to be a very fortunate result. [26]

- The American ambassador to Saigon concluded that "Tet was a massive defeat for the other side, but a psychological victory." [27]

The retaking of Hue by the American forces came too late for many South Vietnamese civilians who were executed as collaborators; some were buried alive.

3
A GUERRILLA WAR
Guerrilla warfare

THE VIETNAM WAR was mostly a guerrilla campaign, a form of fighting that had been part of the Vietnamese tradition for a thousand years. Guerrilla fighters are indistinguishable from ordinary civilians; they wear no uniforms or badges of rank and melt into the community when an attack is over. A North Vietnamese guerrilla commented that in the jungle "we used trees as camouflage" but in the towns "we used people to camouflage us."[28]

The Americans drafted more and more GIs into Vietnam to fight the guerrillas: there were 184,300 in December 1965, nearly 400,000 in 1966 and almost 500,000 in 1967. These men were not ready for bush and jungle warfare. A United States officer, Captain Jim Webb, stated:

> *I had three hot meals in nine months. I carried my pack – it had a poncho, a toothbrush, letter-writing gear and that was it . . . We moved every two days; didn't take a bath for months . . . We ate C-rations continually. And virtually every single person in my unit got either ringworm, hookworm, dysentery or malaria. And some of us had them all.*[29]

A memorial honoring the U.S. paratroopers killed during battles at Chu Lai, South Vietnam, in 1967.

A guerrilla war

A North Vietnamese soldier reveals the entrance to a tunnel used as a hiding place by Vietcong guerrillas.

Were the Vietcong any better off? One of their guerrilla leaders recalled:

> We had to live in miserable conditions in the jungle. We were cold, wet, caught malaria, and did not have enough food when the supply section was delayed or disrupted. For example for three months we had no rice. So we had to eat leaves and roots in the jungle – whatever we could find for survival.[30]

However, the Vietcong had the advantage of long experience in jungle warfare, and they could hide among Vietnamese civilians.

At first, the Americans adopted aggressive "search and destroy" tactics while the Vietcong preferred to "hide, wait and kill." A South Vietnamese wrote:

> The enemy does not confront you. But he harasses you every night to give you the impression that all the people around you are hostile. Everybody becomes your enemy. But in reality it is only the same five or six VC who come back every night.[31]

Gradually, the Americans learned their lesson and set up mixed groups of highly trained Vietnamese and Americans to fight the Vietcong on their own terms. Toward the end of the American phase of the Vietnam conflict, both sides were "hiding and searching," so it became a true jungle war. As an American commander put it, "No one believes in 'search and destroy' but let's do whatever is necessary to do the job so that we can get back home safely."[32]

23

A soldier's lot...

Soldiers can keep up their morale only if they are inspired by patriotism or a passionate belief in their cause. North Vietnamese and Vietcong troops were determined to free their country from foreign intervention, and they were educated in communist beliefs. The Americans had been brought up to believe that communism was threatening to take over the world.

The average age of an American soldier in an infantry unit in Vietnam was nineteen. The GIs were mainly from working-class backgrounds. Many were black, coming from the most downtrodden section of American society. They were given little basic information about the people they were fighting and saw the Vietnamese as "primitive" communist fanatics. An American Marine remembered the daily drill:

> We'd run PT in the morning and every time your left foot hit the deck, you'd have to chant "kill, kill, kill." [33]

The soldier was to become a killing machine.

Survival in war depends upon the cooperation of small groups. The North Vietnamese and Vietcong had a long experience of opposing foreign intervention. The communists divided their companies into three-person cells who took responsibility for each other. The communist cadres ate and slept with the ordinary soldiers, and they all debated operational plans together. There were self-criticism sessions. A North Vietnamese sergeant said his company's discipline always improved after these. A private stated: "We always knew why we were fighting." [34]

From 1968 onward the American GIs began to lose their morale, mainly because of the poor conditions under which they were fighting and the rising level of casualties. There was a breakdown in military discipline and morale, which led to "fragging" – attacks on unpopular officers. Between 1969 and 1971 heroin users rose from 2 percent to 22 percent of the forces.

The American soldiers became lonely and disorientated, fighting in a foreign land. One soldier explained: "I found that even my fellow soldiers had no real interest in my welfare." [35] Many inexperienced GIs were killed

A Vietcong unit in South Vietnam, 1970, engaged in discussion of the latest news.

A heavily armed "grunt" [American soldier] day dreams. His helmet says it all: "Gooks go home." "Born by accident" illustrates the disillusionment of war.

within days of arriving in Vietnam. "I saw my buddies blown away," lamented one Marine, "I never saw a Vietcong." [36]

Doubt entered the minds of many American soldiers. As one said, "After a few months it began to seem crazy... Maybe we shouldn't be in Vietnam." The main thing was to get through the year's tour of service and "go home and forget the whole thing. That's the way you operated." [37]

Both sides suffered heavy casualties. During 1969, an average eight hundred American soldiers were killed and a further six thousand wounded each month. South Vietnamese and communist casualties were much higher. North Vietnamese morale remained high. A private testified to this:

> *Twelve of the eighteen men in our company were killed during an enemy sweep... but we survivors weren't scared... because of the way the cadre had motivated us.* [38]

In contrast to the Vietcong, the American troops, confused and far from home, had difficulty maintaining morale.

Hunters and killers

The Vietnam conflict saw the development of high-tech supersonic air warfare. The Americans and their allies used huge B-52 bombers, supported by supersonic fighters, to bomb North Vietnam. The North Vietnamese depended upon their Soviet and Chinese allies for both airplanes and pilot training. Unlike their enemies, the communist pilots only received crash courses in their Soviet Mig-17s before being committed to battle.

The Migs were smaller and slower than the opposing Sabers and Phantoms but enjoyed greater maneuverability. The communists used their airplanes mainly as interceptors to break up the numerically superior U.S. bomber and fighter formations. As a result their airborne tactics resembled those on the ground. They launched hit and run raids from their airfields around Hanoi and Haiphong rather than attacking in force. In spite of the numerical and technical inferiority of the communists' planes, the early warning provided by the Soviet-made ground control radar systems enabled them to destroy many of the enemy aircraft.

The air war was transformed in July 1965 by the introduction of Surface-to-Air-Missiles (SAMs) and Air-to-Air Missiles (AAMs). The U.S. and Soviet missiles were guided to their targets by sophisticated radar systems.

U.S. military scientists quickly developed direction-finding radar receivers and installed them in their airplanes. American Weasel Sabers located hostile radar systems, and hunter-killer formations of U.S. F-105 fighter-bombers attacked communist SAM batteries with iron bombs, rockets and cannonfire. The North Vietnamese retaliated by ringing their installations with computer-controlled anti-aircraft guns.

The combination of sophisticated surveillance and weapons systems led to highly effective U.S. air attacks. North Vietnamese units moving along the Ho Chi Minh Trail were continually attacked. As one American soldier reported:

All you saw was the air ripped apart and the ground tremoring underneath you. You weren't aware of where the planes had been, yet it was happening yards from our front lines. [39]

Although the North Vietnamese were re-equipped with more advanced Mig 21s, the United States and South Vietnam established complete control of the skies above Vietnam. Their airplanes were faster, more heavily armed and more numerous than those of the communists.

North Vietnamese women, using anti-aircraft machine-guns, prepare to do battle with U.S. aircraft.

A guerrilla war

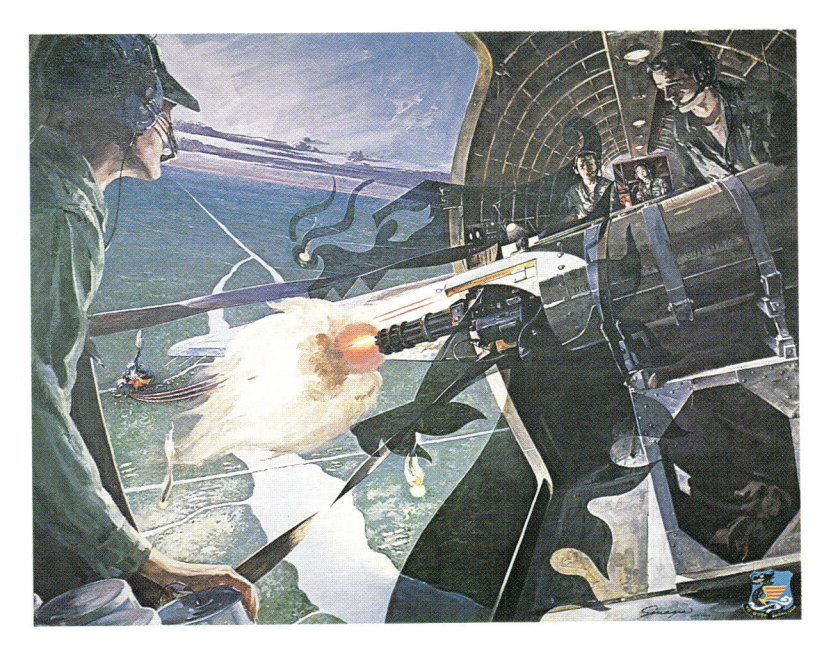

An artist's impression of action on a United States gunship.

Moreover, the South Vietnamese air force was enlarged until it was the fourth largest in the world with 2,075 aircraft and 61,147 officers and men. Even when the United States withdrew from the war, their Southern allies still dominated the air.

High technology, as well as sheer quantity, made the difference between the allied and communist air forces. The allies were able to dominate the skies above Vietnam.

The ruins of Bach Mai Hospital, Hanoi, show vividly the damage caused by B-52 bombers.

The electronic battlefield

The communist guerrillas in Vietnam had great advantages. They were able to build up their forces secretly and attack targets where they enjoyed numerical advantage over their opponents. What could the Americans do to counteract such tactics? Mobility in the form of helicopters offered hope of a solution.

As soon as the Vietcong attacked a position, the U.S. forces launched wave after wave of helicopter gunships. With machine guns mounted in the nose, in belly pods and in open doorways, these flying tanks screamed into action at speeds of up to about 186 mph (300 kph). Behind the gunships came large troop- and munitions-carrying helicopters, which quickly restored U.S. numerical superiority and removed the wounded and dead. These choppers gave the allies the mobility they needed to counteract surprise guerrilla attacks on the ground.

Later models were masterpieces of sophistication with computer-controlled gun-aiming mechanisms and night vision sensors that enabled them to lock onto targets in poor light and deliver telling assaults with missiles, rockets and quick-firing cannon. The U.S. forces gradually created an "electronic" battlefield. Seismic sensors disguised to look like tiny plants were dropped into communist controlled areas where they registered the movements made by men and machines. These signals were relayed to distant computers whose instant print-outs provided helicopter pilots with the coordinates of where to find the enemy. This early intelligence meant that helicopters could adopt an

An American helicopter passing over a village in the mountainous area of north central Vietnam.

U.S. troops moving a wounded comrade to a helicopter to be airlifted to hospital.

offensive as well as a defensive role.

Helicopters also played an important part in urban warfare. They were used to monitor enemy movements through the streets and to bombard guerrillas from the air. The U.S. troops were ferried by helicopter and landed on housetops close to the scene of battle.

Helicopters were susceptible to attack. They were at their most effective when diving down to spray the jungle or streets with bullets but were extremely vulnerable on the turn when enemy machine-gunners had the opportunity to direct their fire on the almost defenseless choppers. The U.S. forces tried to overcome this problem by organizing choppers in formations providing cooperative support and defense. However, there was no defense against ground-to-air missiles, which took a heavy toll of U.S. helicopters.

These unromantic helicopters were so vital to the American war effort that they inspired many war correspondents to sing their praises. According to Michael Herr, a helicopter was

> ... saver-destroyer, provider-waster, right hand-left hand, nimble, fluent, canny and human; hot steel, grease, jungle-saturated canvas webbing, sweat cooling and warming again, cassette rock'n'roll in one ear and door-gun in the other.[40]

Nevertheless, all this advanced technology could not win the war for the United States.

4
TERROR AND ATROCITIES
War crimes

THE VIETNAM WAR was marked by the brutality shown by both sides. Between 1965 and 1973, 201 U.S. army soldiers and 77 Marines were court-martialed for serious crimes against Vietnamese civilians. Although most soldiers did not commit atrocities, there were numerous "cases of women and children being (deliberately) run down by tanks, of GIs picking off children as they ran out to pick up food cartons from an overturned truck, of pilots inviting passengers for human 'turkey shoots'." [41]

The Vietcong used violence to control the Vietnamese population, especially in the South. Thousands of civil servants, police officers, teachers and priests who refused to collaborate with them were murdered. During 1969 alone, about 250 civilians were assassinated or kidnapped each week.

The use of terror spread fear and hatred, creating an environment of atrocity.

In March 1968, U.S. Lieutenant W.L. Calley led a platoon of thirty men into the village of Mylai, where they slaughtered between two hundred and five hundred unarmed villagers:

> *Several old men were stabbed with bayonets, and one was thrown down a well to be followed by a hand grenade. Some women and children praying outside of the local temple were killed by shooting them in the back of the head with rifles.* [42]

The Vietcong were guilty of similar massacres. In 1967, for instance, they attacked the

During a Vietcong attack on Da Nang air base in March 1967, forty-seven people were killed.

Terror and atrocities

TRIAL ORDERED IN CIVILIAN MASSACRE

Officer Charged With Murder of Viet Men, Women, Children

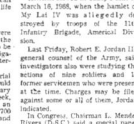

In November 1969 it was announced that Lieutenant Calley would be court-martialed for the premeditated murder of 109 South Vietnamese men, women and children, including a two-year-old. The other twenty-four men who were charged with him were found not guilty. Calley spent just three days in a military jail and was then transferred to house arrest for three and a half years. He was eventually given parole.

South Vietnamese village of Dak Son, spraying the huts with flamethrowers and burning more than 250 villagers alive. Sixty survivors were lined up and shot dead.

Both sides employed highly trained Special Forces to raid enemy territory and to set up spy networks and resistance groups. Nguyen Tuong Lai, a North Vietnamese commander of a Special Forces unit, declared:

> My greatest victory was to kill a priest. We believed he was an intelligence officer. I put an antitank mine in his car on a Sunday morning before he went to perform a church service.[43]

The commander was not the only one with this cold-blooded attitude.

Why did the troops on both sides behave in this way? The war was fought by teenagers: the average age of American combat troops was nineteen, and that of the communists was probably lower. The communists were trained to be ruthless and to make whatever sacrifices in lives – their own and those of the enemy – were necessary to achieve their objective. The U.S. soldiers were trained to hate the Vietnamese; Marine medic Jack McCloskey said he was taught that " . . . anything with slant eyes was a 'gook' – they were not human beings."[44] One American soldier looked at it this way: "We took too many casualties; somebody had to pay."[45]

31

Chemical warfare

The luxuriant forests that covered much of Vietnam provided ideal camouflage for the communist guerrillas. Even with reconnaissance airplanes and helicopters, the Americans and South Vietnamese had difficulty plotting enemy movements. A radical solution was to strip the trees of their foliage. As early as 1961, President Kennedy approved Operation Ranch Hand:

a carefully controlled program of defoliant operations in Vietnam starting with the clearance of key routes and proceeding thereafter to food denial. [46]

This was a controversial decision. Some Americans thought it was a legitimate

▶ Before and After: The top picture shows a South Vietnamese mangrove forest, which was sprayed with Agent Orange in 1965. The bottom photo was taken in 1970: the black patches show surviving trees.

▼ This Vietnamese child was burned by napalm when U.S. air force bombers attacked his village, where guerrillas were thought to be hiding.

Herbicides stripped these trees, leaving nothing but their dead trunks.

strategy in a total war situation; others felt it was unacceptable under any circumstances. It is hard to imagine the wider effects of defoliation on the environment and agriculture. In 1966, 850,000 acres of forest and crops were destroyed by chemical sprays. By 1971, when Operation Ranch Hand was halted, nearly 5.5 million acres of South Vietnamese forest and cropland had been sprayed with herbicides at least once. Particular efforts were made to expose the Ho Chi Minh Trail along which the communists passed reinforcements and munitions. A North Vietnamese recalled:

> *I gradually realized that almost no part of this road was well concealed. Along the roadside, trees had been stripped of leaves and branches. There remained only bare trunks with pointed tops. I was told that on certain days aggressor aircraft, in formations of three, sprayed toxic chemicals over this road. At night dozens of fires flicker on the crests of the hills where the broken remnants of the forest go on burning from one raid to the next.*[47]

This policy failed to stop the guerrillas, so U.S. military scientists undertook to create chemicals that would turn the moist forest earth into slippery grease. Fortunately, Operation Lava, as it was called, was never carried out. Chemical warfare had appalling effects. The defoliant, Agent Orange, contained dioxin, a highly poisonous substance, which built up in the silt of stream beds and entered the ecosystem of Vietnam. The Tu Du Hospital in Saigon received many women suffering from cancers of the womb and many who gave birth to babies with grotesque abnormalities caused by this chemical.

Thousands of soldiers who were exposed to Agent Orange developed cancer and skin diseases. Chemical warfare was not new. It was initially used during World War I, when many were killed or badly injured by mustard gas. More recently, it was used with devastating effects in the Iran-Iraq (1980–88) and the Soviet-Afghan (1979–88) wars.

South Vietnam at war

Life in South Vietnam was affected as much by the presence of the American troops as by the civil war between the government and the Vietcong.

Hundreds of thousands of Vietnamese were employed by the U.S. military, building military bases and hotels or working as house servants and cleaners. In 1966 an estimated thirty thousand orphan girls were working as prostitutes. The Vietnamese drug industry, based on opium, had flourished before the war; but now American soldiers introduced marijuana and heroin. They flooded the cities with their popular culture of Western clothes and juke box music, just as the French colonists had brought their own way of life.

The Vietnamese were amazed by the untold wealth brought by the Americans – everything from cars, to cement for construction, to beer. The cost of living rose as the dollars flooded in, but the value of earnings fell, causing poverty and distress. Modern skyscrapers were built side by side with the colonial shanty towns, from which epidemics of typhoid and bubonic plague spread to rich and poor alike.

This Buddhist priest was one of many who burned themselves to death in Saigon as a protest against what they believed to be the persecution of their faith by the South Vietnamese government.

Terror and atrocities

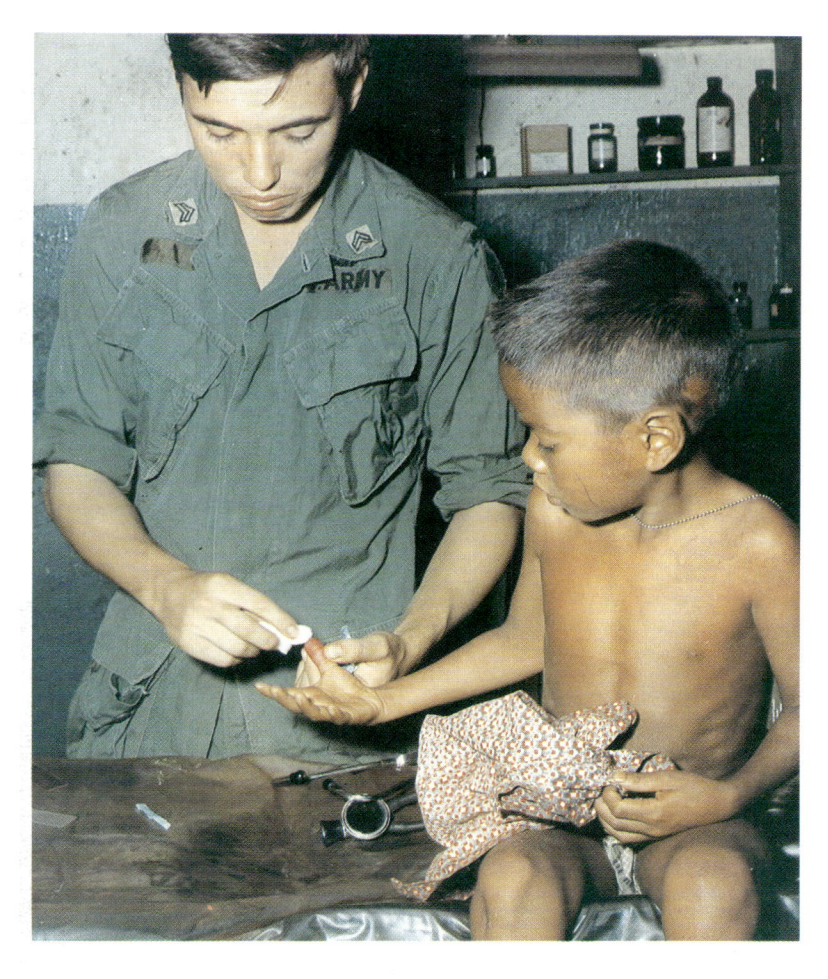

▲ This North Vietnamese propaganda poster shows U.S. dollars linking the unpopular President Thieu to the new military regime in Chile, 1973.

◄ An American medical orderly preparing a blood smear to test a Vietnamese child for malaria.

As they had done in North Vietnam, the United States pursued a policy of "carrot and stick" to gain support. The "carrot" was the Civil Operations and Rural Development Support (CORDS) plan. Introduced in mid-1967, CORDS was intended to win the "hearts and minds" of the villagers away from the Vietcong. Fifty-nine-man teams were sent out to the villages to show the villagers how to defend themselves and to help them improve their housing, sanitation and agriculture. Economic aid totaled $1.7 billion. Thousands of tons of rice, soybean seeds, cooking oil, fertilizers and medicines were distributed.

The CORDS plan alone, however, failed to destroy the Vietcong. Robert Komer, who had developed the CORDS program, started to question it:

> *How can you revive the civil economy and improve the standard of living when the Vietcong are blowing up the roads and bridges?* [48]

In the end, the CORDS policy was unsuccessful.

The "stick" was Operation Phoenix, introduced in 1968. Controlled by an American covert operations group, it aimed to root out Vietcong agents in the rural areas. The U.S.-backed village authorities, who had monthly quotas to fulfill, rounded up as many "suspects" as possible. Most of them were not Vietcong members. Some suffered extreme torture at the hands of their captors, and by late 1970, about twenty thousand suspects had been killed. [49]

North Vietnam at war

Although between 1965 and 1968 the North was subjected to the most intensive bombing the world had ever seen, the Vietcong were not defeated. The secret of their resistance lay in the adaptability of Vietnamese society and in the military and economic aid they received from the Soviet Union and China.

The basic aim of the United States was to interrupt the flow of people and equipment down the Ho Chi Minh Trail. However, each time bridges, roads and rail lines were bombed, "shock brigades" of civilians went to repair them.

A left-wing Australian journalist, Wilfred Burchett, was the only Western journalist to report from the Vietcong's side. He discovered that Vietnamese women knew how to handle guns and that they made up at least half of the local village self-defense units. Some 70 percent of the work force in agriculture and industry were women.

These extracts from Burchett's writing show something about how North Vietnamese society coped with the war.

> *It was compulsory for the kids to wear green camouflage when they attended school . . . I remember once driving through an area and to my great astonishment the whole field of maize suddenly got to its feet and charged across the road.* [50]

> *. . . the "city" of Vinh Linh [was] a complex of villages, which had burrowed thirty feet beneath its former location . . . linked by tunnels, this community was officially said to number seventy thousand people and to extend for several hundred kilometers. For successive years these people tended the crop-land and repaired the border supply routes at night . . .* [51]

Vietcong guerrillas cut the enemy's lines, knowing that effective communications were essential to the American and South Vietnamese war effort.

Terror and atrocities

North Vietnamese children wearing straw hats, used for camouflage.

Although the total commitment of the people to the war effort was very important, it would have been severely hampered without aid from the Soviet Union and China, which overcame scarcities of food and other commodities. The rail lines were constantly being repaired by Chinese laborers to enable the free flow of goods southward.

After the halt in the bombing in November 1968 the North Vietnamese began to rebuild:

> *Everywhere the landscape gleamed with the bright red of brick and tile – new homes, schools, factories standing out like beacons in towns which had seemed permanently extinguished.* [52]

Red banners hung everywhere proclaiming the word "Vigilance." It was expected that the bombers would return. Very soon they did. President Richard Nixon would carry the war policy forward and strike at Cambodia and Laos as well.

These women remained armed at all times.

5
A HARD ROAD TO PEACE: 1968–73
Nixon's war

AFTER WINNING THE PRESIDENCY in 1968 with the promise of peace, Richard Nixon faced a difficult situation. The heavy casualties resulting from the Tet Offensive had boosted opposition to the war at home and abroad. In the face of widespread demands for peace, Nixon responded with a new policy:
- U.S. troop strength was reduced.
- Secret peace talks with the communists were started.
- The South Vietnamese army was greatly enlarged to compensate for the reduced American forces, a policy called "Vietnamization."

Nixon was determined to obtain what he described as "peace with honor" – the communists had to make concessions. When the peace talks languished, Nixon authorized the United States air force to bomb Cambodia because it allowed Vietcong troops to pass through its territory. A year later, in April 1970, he ordered U.S. troops into Cambodia to destroy the "sanctuaries" – the strongholds held by the communists there. Lon Nol, the ruler of Cambodia, had not been consulted. Alexander Haig (at that time deputy to Presidential Assistant Henry Kissinger) defended these attacks upon a neutral country, saying that "we had every right legally and morally to take what action was necessary to protect our forces." [53]

A CBS opinion poll showed that the American public supported the Cambodian invasion by two to one. But a subsequent Gallup poll showed that 48 percent favored the immediate withdrawal of United States troops from Vietnam, or at least by mid-1971, while 31 percent supported withdrawal over as long a time as necessary. [54]

Undeterred, the North Vietnamese streamed down the Ho Chi Minh Trail, and the Americans found themselves facing major opposition for the first time in two years. In January 1971 Nixon ordered the invasion of Laos by South Vietnamese troops, supported by U.S. artillery, airplanes and helicopters. They were repelled by the communists.

The news of the defeat was greeted with fury in the United States, especially as the

Richard Nixon celebrating his victory in the 1968 presidential election.

A hard road to peace 1968–73

This North Vietnamese propaganda poster of U.S. pilots in captivity was intended to arouse American anti-war sentiment.

publication of the confidential "classified" Pentagon Papers exposed the "entire history of deception and misjudgment involving successive presidents"[55] during the war in Vietnam. Encouraged by the social disturbances in America and knowing that Nixon needed success to be reelected to the presidency, the communists launched the Spring Offensive in 1972. They believed that military success would bring them stronger negotiating powers. Nixon retaliated by ordering massive air strikes against Hanoi and Haiphong and the mining of North Vietnamese ports.

By mid-July, superior U.S. air power had stopped the communists in their tracks, and in November Nixon was reelected. When the communists proved slow to negotiate, Nixon ordered the continuous bombing of Hanoi and Haiphong for eleven days. This brought the communists to the diplomatic table. Ceasefire agreements were formally signed in Paris on January 27, 1973. Within six weeks, the last American soldier had left Vietnam.

Nixon claimed: "We have finally achieved 'peace with honor'." Nixon's critics claimed that the bombing and invasions of Cambodia and Laos, with the resulting hundreds of thousands of casualties, gained nothing. "Peace with honor" had little real meaning for the United States or Vietnam.

"Hell no, we won't go!"

At an anti-war rally in 1968, after the Tet Offensive,

> ...a bloodied, beaten-up anti-war demonstrator shinnied up the flagpole and replaced the American flag with his bloodied shirt, saying, "let the world see what's happening in Chicago."

At this point the police charged the crowd, swinging their clubs and shouting "Kill. Kill. Kill."[56] This extract suggests the nature of official reactions to the anti-war protests.

The opinion polls showed that the majority of Americans supported the war until the horrific news films of the Tet Offensive shook their confidence. There were other reasons too, as the following statistics show.

David Dellinger, a lifelong pacifist, said the people demanded an end to the war when casualties mounted and "GIs started coming home in canvas bags."[58]

Another reason was social strife in the United States. Many Americans supported the civil rights movement led by Martin Luther King, which demanded equality for black people. An important issue in the campaign was the military draft. College students, who generally came from affluent families, did not have to serve in Vietnam, while poorer people – including many blacks – were drafted. Research showed that twice as many black soldiers were given combat assignments as whites.[59] Thus the struggle for equal rights for black people played its part in the anti-war movement.

	American troops in Vietnam	American deaths in Vietnam
1965	180,000	1,728
1966	380,000	6,053
1967	450,000	11,058
1968	540,000	17,622
1969	543,000	11,527
1970	280,000	6,065
1971	140,000	2,348
1972	70,000	561
TOTAL		56,962[57]

These statistics tell much of the story of American involvement in Vietnam.
The low casualty figure for 1965 escalated rapidly, peaking in 1968, the year of the Tet Offensive.
The steep decline in deaths from 1970 onward reflects the progressive withdrawal of U.S. troops and the superiority of U.S. power.

Many young people refused to be drafted into the armed forces; an estimated 250,000 avoided registration. A large number took refuge in Europe and Canada, where they participated in huge demonstrations against United States involvement in Vietnam.

Every military campaign after the Tet Offensive generated protests that often led to violence. The worst incident took place at Kent State University, Ohio, in May 1970, following the American invasion of Cambodia. Four students were shot dead by police during a demonstration. Within days, a great number of colleges struck in protest.

A hard road to peace 1968–73

◀ There were demonstrations against the Vietnam War in many countries, including Britain. This protest in London took place in October 1967.

▼ This anti-war poster, which satirizes a famous World War I recruitment advertisement, shows a wounded Uncle Sam appealing for the Americans to leave Vietnam.

What effect did the anti-war movement have? Secretary of State Dean Rusk believed that it persuaded the North Vietnamese "not to try to find a peaceful solution but to persist and win politically what they could not win militarily." [60] This view was supported from the other side by the former Vietcong leader, Truong Nhu Tang. Many of those who led the anti-war movement judged that it had a minimal effect. Eugene McCarthy, one of the movement's leaders, argued:

> *The war would have ended just about when it did, even if there had been no protest . . . because they didn't end it on policy finally, they ended it because they were losing.* [61]

Did the American government end the war merely because it was losing, or had there also been a change of heart in the administration? There is no hard and fast answer. The views of Dean Rusk and Eugene McCarthy on the anti-war movement reflect an ongoing difference of opinion in the American public.

41

Red flag over Saigon

When the Americans left Vietnam, the South Vietnamese had the fourth largest air force in the world and a million men under arms. Thieu's regime controlled about 75 percent of South Vietnam's territory and about 85 percent of its population. With continuing American aid, they seemed easily able to defend themselves. Yet within three years, the South had fallen to the communists. How did this happen? Part of the problem lay with the government of South Vietnam.

Thieu's regime was very weak and inefficient. There were millions of refugees, and many who had worked for the Americans were now unemployed. Instead of trying to broaden support for his government, Thieu cracked down on the opposition. He alienated the peasants by allowing the landlords to recover land that had been divided among landless people. Corruption was still rife. Much of the American aid was siphoned off by Thieu and his ruling circle. An old Vietnamese saying, "A house leaks from the roof," seemed to apply to South Vietnam.

The country was in the grip of galloping inflation: in 1973–4, the prices of rice, sugar, and cooking oil doubled. Despite record harvests, the South had to import large quantities of rice from the United States. Although the country was in chaos, Thieu's priority was to recover land from the communists.

The North Vietnamese were determined to topple Thieu's regime. They constructed a network of roads leading to the frontier, and air defenses were improved. For the first time, they built up formidable tank and armor spearheads with which to meet the enemy on the battlefield. Meanwhile, the communists in the South were increasing their influence.

When fighting broke out again, the United States provided the South with material aid. But it was clear that the majority of Americans would no longer stomach any greater involvement. The South Vietnamese were short

Not all South Vietnamese feared the communist takeover of 1975. These citizens of Hue are holding placards welcoming the communists.

A hard road to peace 1968–73

A helicopter being pushed over the side of an aircraft carrier, to make room for incoming choppers carrying military personnel and their families, escaping from South Vietnam as the communist armies approached.

of ammunition, spare parts and medicines, and the army's morale crumbled. Early in 1975, the South's resistance collapsed, President Thieu resigned, and the communists entered Saigon in triumph.

Many South Vietnamese feared that the communist takeover would lead to the bloody massacre of all who had been involved with the old regime. Bui Tin, a senior North Vietnamese journalist, tried to allay their fears:

> *You have nothing to fear. Between Vietnamese, there are no victors and no vanquished. Only the Americans have been beaten. If you are patriots, consider this a moment of joy.* [62]

It was understandably hard for many South Vietnamese to believe his words. But as it happened there was no bloodbath; the South Vietnamese government had totally surrendered to the communists and further fighting was unnecessary. The remaining few thousand Americans in Saigon watched as "eight years of American combat was rendered meaningless in as many weeks."[63] Then they were hurriedly evacuated by the last United States Marines to enter Vietnam.

6
THE LEGACY OF VIETNAM
A poor country

THE VIETNAM WAR left "at least one dead, or some wounded, in each Vietnamese family,"[64] according to one communist officer. In 1975, in South Vietnam alone, there were one million widows and 800,000 children who had been orphaned or abandoned, mainly by fathers who were U.S. soldiers.

Some 200,000 senior South Vietnamese military officers and officials were placed in "reeducation camps" where they worked all day and received political indoctrination in the evenings. Prisoners who asked questions were sent to the "discipline house" where they were "put in chains for many months and not permitted to see the daylight."[65] "They controlled our lives," said an ex-prisoner, "by the threat of starvation."[66] Many prisoners died of disease and malnutrition. As late as 1983, 63,000 were still in prison.

The huge task of reconstruction began immediately. The country was desperately short of materials; resourceful people adapted the wreckage of tanks and airplanes for use in rebuilding factories and schools. All land was taken over by the state, and the farmers had to work on collective farms. The government appropriated more than five hundred factories in the South, producing textiles, chemicals, paper and food products. The development of heavy industry took priority over the production of consumer goods.

More than one hundred nations established diplomatic relations with the new Vietnamese government. The United States was the one major country to withhold such recognition. Some countries, such as Sweden, Australia and the Soviet Union, provided generous aid, but the United States government refused any assistance.

Attempts at rapid economic development proved unsuccessful, hampered by insufficient foreign aid and by domestic mismanagement. The skills of many professionals, interned in the reeducation camps, were wasted. Regional differences between the North and the South complicated matters further. The North Vietnamese, used to spartan conditions endured during thirty years of wartime, were contemptuous of the relative wealth of the South. They tried to stamp out

Some of these children in an orphanage in Ho Chi Minh City [Saigon] had American soldier fathers. At first, the communist authorities had difficulty deciding how such children should be treated.

The legacy of Vietnam

▲ Thousands of Vietnamese fled from communist Vietnam and sought refuge in other Asian and Western states. A few were accepted, but the majority were interned in camps.

◀ Bach Mai Hospital, Hanoi, being rebuilt after the war.

the bars and the drug trade, the symbols of "Western decadence," but with only moderate success. Many from the North were attracted to the popular culture of Saigon, now renamed Ho Chi Minh City.

In 1975 about 230,000 South Vietnamese left the country to settle in the United States and Canada.[67] The flow of refugees increased in 1978 when the government introduced restrictions on the trading activities of the Hoa, the Chinese community in Vietnam. The refugees left Vietnam in crowded ships, and they became known as the "boat people." They left, as did other Vietnamese, mainly to escape the cycle of poverty.

Vietnam remained one of the poorest countries in the world, still barely self-sufficient in food in 1990.

Censorship and war

Most governments censor information given to their people during a war to deny the enemy any advantage that might arise from their victories or from problems developing on the home front.

At the beginning of the Vietnam War, the United States government respected the rights of the free press and trusted the newspapers and television companies to regulate the news in the best interests of the state. But this was the first televised war, bringing uncensored images to the public instantaneously, and it had unexpected results. As the horrors of the Tet Offensive flashed onto their television screens, Americans were deeply shocked and began to question their involvement in the war. General Westmoreland complained bitterly that "doom and gloom reporting" destroyed public morale. Secretary of State Dean Rusk accused the press of sabotaging the war efforts:

> *I think we helped to persuade the North Vietnamese to persist and to me that is a tragedy.* [68]

On the other hand, Eric Sevareid, a television news commentator, argued:

This poster, "War's First Casualty," was produced during World War II.

The legacy of Vietnam

This North Vietnamese poster, captioned "Better Death than Slavery," portrays the determination of the Vietnamese people.

It is true, however, that Americans received a largely uncensored view of the war.

In sharp contrast, the North Vietnamese government exercised iron control over all forms of mass media, which maintained a remorseless attack upon the United States. Posters and murals were skillfully used – boldly painted heroic scenes with captions such as "Uncle Ho is still marching with us" and pictures of destruction dominated by a huge coffin entitled "Nixon's doctrine." The propaganda was aimed at helping the communists to keep up their people's morale.

Censorship during war is always a contentious issue. Following are some of the important questions now subject to debate:

- Should there be freedom of the press, or should the government control the media to prevent the enemy from gaining important information?
- Is it possible to maintain support for a war, simply by preventing the public from finding out the negative side of the war effort?
- Are there certain matters, such as military secrets, that should be censored in wartime, and how is it possible to decide where to draw the line?
- Should live, uncensored television pictures and war reports be permitted?

> *I'm sure that Hanoi kept a very close watch on press coverage . . . But the activity they had to respond to was in front of them – a constant reinforcement of the American air force, infantry, artillery, navy, everything else.* [69]

This satirical cartoon is from the British *Daily Telegraph* in 1970.

How was a superpower beaten?

No sooner was the Vietnam War over, than all kinds of people from soldiers to academics began to ask how the most powerful nation in the world could have been defeated.

Secretary of State Dean Rusk argued that perhaps "President Kennedy should have put in a hundred thousand troops immediately."[70] General Westmoreland blamed President Johnson for not allowing him to invade North Vietnam, and he criticized the South Vietnamese for their lack of "fighting spirit." Keegan, another American general, asserted that the Americans had provided the South Vietnamese army with "the wrong equipment, wrong tactics and maybe wrong doctrines."[71]

General Van Tien Dung, the North Vietnamese commander during the later stages of the war, believed that the American soldiers never really adapted themselves to guerrilla warfare:

> *They applied a lot of new strategies such as "Special War," "Local War" and "Vietnamization," but the result of it all was the biggest failure in the history of the United States.*[72]

The debate ranged over political as well as military matters. The U.S. government had aimed to destroy the communists, but instead communist power had grown. The United States misunderstood the nature of Vietnamese nationalism; the more bombs were dropped, the more people flocked to the communist-led resistance. If Dean Rusk's policy of maximum force at the beginning had been followed, it might have won the war, but that is far from certain.

Some critics went even further to suggest that "the Vietnam War represents not only a political mistake and a national defeat but also a moral failure."[73] The debate among academics continued for several years. Paul Kattenberg wrote:

> *The morality of the U.S. involvement must . . . be judged in terms of its ultimate results. Did the United States by intervening mitigate [prevent] more pain and suffering than it caused by intervening, or than would have resulted if it had not intervened?*[74]

James Fallows, writing in the *New York Times* argued that:

> *If American presidents meant well at the beginning, the ensuing chain of consequences is legitimized by their good intent.*[75]

Attacks by South Vietnamese troops on villages such as this one led many people to support the communists.

The legacy of Vietnam

This question of morality will be argued for years to come: was it right for the United States to intervene in another country that was fighting for its independence, because it felt threatened by communism?

▲ The Vietnam memorial in Washington D.C. was unveiled in November 1982. It lists all the Americans who died in the Vietnam War.

▶ A Vietnamese man examines a tank abandoned at the end of the war.

Lessons learned?

The experience of the Vietnam War not only affected the inhabitants of Indochina and the United States, but also influenced events across the world.

One horrific casualty of the war was Cambodia, which was convulsed by civil war following the U.S.-backed invasion of 1970. In 1975 the Khmer Rouge, a communist party supported by China, seized power and attempted an instant peasant revolution. The changes were forced through with great brutality, and one-quarter of the population is estimated to have perished in the process.

Future United States foreign policy was haunted by the ghost of Vietnam. Heed was taken of the warning from a former State Department policy maker "not to mess into other people's civil wars where there is no substantial American strategic interest at stake."[76] The United States became less willing to engage in full-scale military involvement in foreign countries, preferring lightning actions to achieve specific goals, for example, bombing Libya in 1986 and invading Grenada (1984) and Panama (1989).

The Soviet Union experienced the "Vietnam syndrome" when it occupied Afghanistan in 1979, discovering how difficult it is even for a great power to defeat determined guerrilla forces in difficult terrain. Soviet forces were forced to withdraw in 1988.

The British government, having seen how live television coverage of the Vietnam War had led to outrage in the United States, realized the advantages of controlling the media during wartime.

Phnom Penh, the capital of Cambodia, in October 1979. People were gradually returning to the city, deserted for four years after its enforced evacuation by the regime.

The legacy of Vietnam

The cast of *Platoon*, a powerful American movie about the Vietnam War, written and directed by Oliver Stone, a Vietnam veteran.

During the Falklands War between Britain and Argentina in 1982, no immediate television pictures were shown and there were few shots of injured British troops. It was argued that such action was necessary to keep up public support for the war and to deny potentially useful information to the enemy.

Was the legacy of Vietnam enough to prevent a similar war in the future? For several years the guilt the American people felt for their involvement in the war was apparent. In their midst were thousands of Vietnam veterans who were permanently scarred, physically and psychologically, and who found it difficult to return to civilian society. Films were produced showing the horror of the war for both sides, including "Apocalypse Now" and "Born on the Fourth of July," the story of Vietnam veteran Ron Kovic, who was disabled in the conflict. A survey in 1982 showed that more than 70 percent of the American public viewed the war as "fundamentally wrong and immoral."

Yet in 1991 U.S. forces once more became involved in full military conflict in the Gulf War. The ghost of Vietnam, which had been haunting American foreign policy for nearly twenty years, was partially laid to rest.

Leading figures

Ngo Dinh Diem (1901–63)
Diem was born in Annam, the son of a Roman Catholic mandarin. As a civil servant, he refused to cooperate with the Japanese or the French and he lived in exile in the United States between 1950 and 1954. On his return to South Vietnam in 1954, he became prime minister to Bao Dai, whom he ousted the following year. He refused to hold elections in accordance with the Geneva agreement of 1954. Members of Diem's family were hated for their corrupt activities, and his government failed to win popularity. The United States became increasingly critical of his leadership, and in November 1963 he was overthrown and murdered by his generals.

▲ President Diem in 1962.

▶ General Giap in 1984, at the scene of the battle of Dien Bien Phu.

Dwight D. Eisenhower (1890–1969)
Eisenhower was a professional soldier who commanded the United States forces during World War II (1941–45). His greatest success was the 1944 D-Day landings in Normandy, which enabled the Allies to liberate France. He joined the Republican Party and was elected president in 1952. Eisenhower was intensely suspicious of what he regarded as Soviet and Chinese expansionism in Indochina. He developed the "Domino Theory," which suggested that if Indochina fell to the communists, the rest of the Southeast Asian countries would follow like a row of dominoes tumbling one after the other. He backed the French in their struggle with the Vietminh and endorsed support for Diem's government after 1955.

Vo Nguyen Giap (1912–)
Giap was the founder of the Vietminh and its commander-in-chief throughout the wars against the Japanese, French and Americans. Born in Annam, the son of a mandarin, he worked as a lawyer, teacher and journalist.

Lyndon B. Johnson

Giap was imprisoned between 1930 and 1933 for his activities in the Indochinese Communist Party. His sister was executed for political dissent and his wife died in a French jail. When Ho Chi Minh proclaimed the Democratic Republic of Vietnam in 1945, he became its first minister of defense. Giap created the military organization that defeated the French at Dien Bien Phu and developed the guerrilla tactics of the North Vietnamese. He was responsible for the disastrous Tet Offensive of 1968.

Lyndon B. Johnson (1908–1973)

Johnson was a tall Texan who developed into a first-class organizer for the Democratic Party. As vice-president, he assumed the presidency when Kennedy was assassinated in 1963. It was Johnson who first ordered U.S. combat troops to intervene directly in Vietnam. Although a minority of Americans opposed Johnson's intervention policy from the beginning, it was not until the television coverage of the battles during the Tet Offensive of 1968 that the trust of the majority was shaken. Johnson became so disillusioned with the situation in Vietnam that he refused to seek reelection in 1968 and retired to his Texan ranch.

John F. Kennedy (1917–1963)

Kennedy, a Democrat, was one of the most exciting and most skillfully promoted presidents of all time. The product of a politically active family, he was carefully groomed for the presidency after a successful naval career during World War II. In 1960 he defeated Republican opponent Richard Nixon and became the first Roman Catholic president of the United States. He represented the hope that a "New Frontier" would be created in the United States, where discrimination, injustice and poverty would be eliminated. The Vietnam War was a continual worry throughout his short presidency; he could not decide whether to continue to prop up the South Vietnamese regime financially or to send in combat troops. Kennedy was a popular president, and his assassination in November 1963 appalled the nation and the world.

Ho Chi Minh (1890–1969)

Born in central Vietnam as Nguyen Tat Thanh, Ho Chi Minh traveled widely in his youth. He was a founder member of the French Communist Party in 1920, and he worked as a communist organizer after visiting Moscow. He founded the Indochinese Communist Party in 1930. Upon returning to Vietnam in 1941, he established the Vietminh. Ho proclaimed Vietnam's independence at the end of World War II, and as president and premier of North Vietnam, he led the struggle against the French over the next nine years. An able strategist and poet, Ho Chi Minh demonstrated great flexibility of thought and was prepared to cooperate with other parties in his single-minded aim to achieve full independence for his country.

Richard M. Nixon (1913–)

Nixon trained as a lawyer and was elected to the House of Representatives in 1946 where he quickly gained a reputation as a leading anti-communist. After a brief spell as a senator, he became President Eisenhower's vice-president in 1952. Nixon was elected

Ho Chi Minh in 1967.

president in 1968, having pledged to end the Vietnam War. But the war continued until 1973; his critics argued that the terms of the eventual ceasefire were no better than those offered in 1968, and that therefore hundreds of thousands of American and Indochinese lives had been unnecessarily lost. Many of Nixon's policies were as devious as his nickname "Tricky Dick" suggested. The Watergate scandals revealed Nixon's serious personal misconduct, and he was forced to resign in August 1974.

Nguyen Van Thieu (1923–)
Thieu was born in South Vietnam and fought with the Vietminh against the Japanese and the French in the early 1940s. However, he became disillusioned with the communists and switched sides in 1946. In 1964, after the murder of President Diem (in which he was involved), he became chief of staff of the South Vietnamese army. He was elected president in 1967 and remained in office until 1975. Thieu never succeeded in breaking the traditional corruption of the South Vietnamese government or the power of the landlords over the rural areas. He was critical of what he considered to be half-hearted American support during the invasions of Laos and Cambodia. He fled Vietnam shortly before the fall of Saigon to the communists in April 1975 and went to live in Britain.

Harry S. Truman (1884–1972)
Truman, who was born in Independence, Missouri, became a leading Democrat in the 1930s. He became president of the United States in 1945. Truman believed that the United States should support regimes throughout the world against the threat of communism. When communist North Korea invaded South Korea in 1950, he sent U.S. troops to the aid of South Korea. Anxious to prevent any further communist advances, he gave generous aid to the French in their fight against the Vietminh. In 1952, he retired from political life and returned to Missouri.

General Westmoreland in December 1966. At that time he was considered an attractive candidate for the presidency, who would offer decisive leadership in the Vietnam War.

William C. Westmoreland (1914–)
Westmoreland graduated from West Point and served in World War II. After being appointed commander of the American forces in Vietnam (1964–68), he advised President Johnson to escalate the war by pouring forty-four additional combat battalions into Vietnam, but Johnson refused. Westmoreland failed to advise the president of the seriousness of the difficulties facing U.S. troops. In June 1968, he was appointed chairman of the Joint Chiefs of Staff in Washington (1968–72) and was replaced as commander of the American forces in Vietnam by General Creighton W. Abrams. He retired in 1972. Westmoreland played a lively role in the debate over who was responsible for the United States defeat in Vietnam, and in 1976 he published a book called *A Soldier Reports*.

Important dates

Date	Events
1802	Unification of Vietnam.
1857	French forces defeat Vietnamese at Da Nang.
1861	French forces capture Saigon.
1883	French divide Vietnam into Tonkin and Annam protectorates.
1887	French create Indochinese Union, composed of Cochin-China, Annam, Tonkin and Cambodia.
1890	Ho Chi Minh is born.
1893	Laos added to the Indochinese Union.
1920	Ho Chi Minh joins the newly formed French Communist Party.
1924	Ho goes to Moscow.
1930	Ho forms Indochinese Communist Party in Hong Kong.
1932	Bao Dai, theoretically the emperor since 1925, returns to Vietnam to ascend the throne with French support.
1940	Japan occupies Indochina, but leaves the French administration intact.
1941	Ho returns to Vietnam and forms Vietminh with Vo Nguyen Giap.
1944	Giap forms the Vietminh army.
1945	*March* Japanese take over French administration throughout Indochina. Bao Dai proclaims the independence of Vietnam under Japanese auspices. *August* Japan capitulates to the Allies and transfers power to the Vietminh. Bao Dai abdicates and Ho declares Vietnam independent.
1946	*March* France recognizes Vietnam as a "free state" within the French Union. *November* French warships shell Haiphong.
1949	*April* Bao Dai returns to Vietnam. *November* Chinese communists declare the People's Republic of China.
1950	Ho declares that the Democratic Republic of Vietnam is the only legal government.
1953	*October* Laos granted full independence as a member of the French Union. *December* Vietminh forces enter Laos.
1954	The Geneva Conference arranges a ceasefire for Vietnam, Cambodia and Laos.
1955	Ngo Dinh Diem proclaims himself president of the Republic of Vietnam.
1957	Communists begin guerrilla war in the Mekong delta.
1959	North Vietnamese begin to send troops and munitions to the guerrillas in the South down the Ho Chi Minh Trail.
1960	The National Liberation Front for South Vietnam (Vietcong) is formed.
1963	A coup by General Duong Van Minh ousts Ngo Dinh Diem, who is murdered. John F. Kennedy is assassinated, and Lyndon Johnson becomes the U.S. president.
1964	The North Vietnamese attack USNS *Maddox* in the Gulf of Tonkin. Lyndon Johnson wins the U.S. presidential election.
1965	*February* U.S. bombing of North Vietnam begins. *March* The first U.S. combat troops arrive at Da Nang. *June* Air Commodore Nguyen Cao Ky becomes prime minister of South Vietnam.
1966	U.S. forces bomb Hanoi and Haiphong.
1967	Nguyen Van Thieu is elected president of South Vietnam, with Ky as vice-president.
1968	*January* The North Vietnamese and the Vietcong stage the Tet Offensive. *November* Richard Nixon is elected president of the United States.

Date	Events
1969	*March* Nixon orders the secret bombing of Cambodia. *September* Ho Chi Minh dies. *October* Huge anti-war demonstrations in the United States.
1970	*February* Presidential Assistant Henry Kissinger begins secret talks with North Vietnamese negotiator Le Duc Tho. *April* American and South Vietnamese forces attack Cambodia. *May* Four students are killed by police at an anti-war demonstration at Kent State University, Ohio.
1971	*February* South Vietnamese begin incursions into Laos. *June* The "Pentagon Papers" published.
1972	*March* The North Vietnamese launch an offensive across the demilitarized zone. *April* U.S. forces bomb Hanoi and Haiphong. *November* Nixon is reelected president. *December* Talks between Kissinger and Le Duc Tho break down; U.S. forces bomb Hanoi and Haiphong.
1973	*January* A ceasefire is agreed upon. *March* The last U.S. troops leave South Vietnam.
1975	The communists take over the whole of Vietnam.
1977	Vietnam invades Cambodia.
1978	The ethnic Chinese begin to flee Vietnam.
1979	China invades Vietnam.

Glossary

Agent Orange	A poisonous chemical compound used to destroy the foliage of trees.
Allies	In World War II, the Allies were the countries that fought against Germany, Japan and Italy.
Assassination	The planned murder of a prominent public figure.
Body count	A measure of the number of troops and civilians killed during the war.
Bourgeoisie	The middle class. In Marxism, the class opposed to the proletariat, or working class.
Cadre	The professional revolutionaries in a communist organization.
Chopper	An informal name for a helicopter.
CIA	Central Intelligence Agency, responsible for collecting intelligence information on possible enemies of the United States.
Coexistence	Existing together in peace.
Colonist	A person who settles in another country but remains under the political rule of his or her own country.
Commonwealth	An association of sovereign states.
Communism	The political theory of a classless society where private ownership has been abolished, in which each person is provided for according to his or her need.
Containment	The U.S. foreign policy after World War II to prevent the spread of communism.
C-rations	U.S. combat rations consisting of concentrated foods and canned goods.
Defoliants	Chemical herbicides used to destroy vegetation.
Destroyer	A small, fast, lightly armored but heavily armed warship.
Domino Theory	The theory that if Vietnam fell to communism, the other countries of Southeast Asia would follow and fall like a row of dominoes.
Draft	A call-up for compulsory military service.
Dysentery	An infection of the intestine that causes severe diarrhea.
Expansionism	The doctrine or practice of expanding the economy or territory of a country.
Flamethrower	A weapon that ejects a stream or spray of burning fluid.
Guerrilla	A member of an irregular army fighting the regular forces of a state.
Gunship	A combat helicopter, armed with multiple guns and rockets.
High-tech	Advanced technology.
Ho Chi Minh Trail	The route from China down through Laos and Cambodia to South Vietnam.
Howitzer	A type of cannon with a short or medium barrel.
Malaria	A contagious disease caused by the bite of an infected mosquito.
Mandarin	A highly educated, high-ranked Chinese or Vietnamese official.
Mangrove	A tropical evergreen tree or shrub.
Manifesto	A statement of aims and policies by a political party.
Maneuverability	Ability to move around easily.
Mortar	A cannon that fires shells over a short range.
Napalm	A form of jellied gas that sticks and sets fire to anything it touches.
Nationalist	A person who is devoted to his or her country.
Nationalization	The taking over by the state of an industry or service.

Neutral	Not siding with any party to a war or dispute.
Pentagon	The offices of the U.S. Department of Defense. They are built in the form of a pentagon.
Reactionary	A person who is opposed to social change. An extreme conservative.
Reconnaissance	The process of obtaining information about the position and activities of an enemy in wartime.
Seismic sensors	Instruments used to register the movements of people or machines.
Spearhead	The leading force in a military attack.
Strafe	To machine-gun from the air.
Supersonic	Capable of reaching a speed faster than the speed of sound.
Surveillance	Close observation of a person or group.
VC	An abbreviation for Vietcong, used by the Americans.
Vietcong	The nickname for the communist National Liberation Front for South Vietnam.
Vietminh	The Vietnamese nationalist organization, led by the communists, which fought for the independence of Vietnam.

Further reading

Edwards, Richard. *Vietnam War* (Rourke Corporation, 1987)
Fincher, E.B. *The Vietnam War.* (Franklin Watts, 1980)
Kurland, Gerald. *The My Lai Massacre* (SamHar Press, 1973)
Lawson, Don. *An Album of the Vietnam War* (Franklin Watts, 1986)
Lawson, Don. *The United States in the Vietnam War* (Harper & Row, 1981)
Warren, James A. *Portrait of a Tragedy: America and the Vietnam War* (Lothrop, 1989)
Wills, Charles. *The Tet Offensive.* (Silver Burdett Press, 1989)

Notes on sources

1. Cited in Baker, M., *Nam*, William Morrow & Co., 1981.
2. *Ibid.*
3. Cited in Santoli, A., *To Bear Any Burden*, Abacus, 1985.
4. *Ibid.*
5. Cited in Karnow, S., *Vietnam*, Century, 1983.
6. Cited in Maclear, M., *Vietnam: The Ten Thousand Day War*, Thames Hudson, 1981.
7. Karnow, *op. cit.*
8. Cited in Lacouture, T., *Ho Chi Minh*, Penguin, 1967.
9. Karnow, *op. cit.*
10. Cited in Lacouture, *op. cit.*
11. Maclear, *op. cit.*
12. *Ibid.*
13. *Ibid.*
14. *Ibid.*
15. *Ibid.*
16. Santoli, *op. cit.*
17. Maclear, *op. cit.*
18. *Ibid.*
19. *Ibid.*
20. *Ibid.*
21. Karnow, *op. cit.*
22. *Ibid.*
23. Maclear, *op. cit.*
24. *Ibid.*
25. Karnow, *op. cit.*
26. *Ibid.*
27. Maclear, *op. cit.*
28. Santoli, *op. cit.*
29. Maclear, *op. cit.*
30. Santoli, *op. cit.*
31. *Ibid.*
32. Maclear, *op. cit.*
33. Keegan, J., *Soldiers: A History of Men in Battle*, Hamilton, 1985.
34. Karnow, *op. cit.*
35. *Ibid.*
36. Baker, *op. cit.*
37. Karnow, *op. cit.*
38. *Ibid.*
39. Maclear, *op. cit.*
40. Herr, M., *Dispatches*, Picador, 1978.
41. Santoli, *op. cit.*
42. Walton, G., *The Tarnished Shield*, Dodd, 1973.
43. Santoli, *op. cit.*
44. Maclear, *op. cit.*
45. Doyle, E., & Weiss, S., *A Collision of Cultures*, Boston Publishing Co., 1985.
46. Maclear, *op. cit.*
47. *Ibid.*
48. *Ibid.*
49. *Ibid.*
50. Cited in Maclear, *op. cit.*
51. Cited in *ibid.*
52. *Ibid.*
53. *Ibid.*
54. *Ibid.*
55. *Ibid.*
56. *Ibid.*
57. *U.S. Casualties in South East Asia*, U.S. Department of Defense, Washington, 1985.
58. Cited in Maclear, *op. cit.*
59. *Ibid.*
60. *Ibid.*
61. *Ibid.*
62. Karnow, *op. cit.*
63. Maclear, *op. cit.*
64. Doyle, E., & Maitland, T., *The Aftermath*, Boston Publishing Co., 1985.
65. Santoli, *op. cit.*
66. *Ibid.*
67. Maclear, *op. cit.*
68. Maclear, *op. cit.*
69. Lipsman, S., & Weiss, S., *False Peace*, Boston Publishing Co., 1985.
70. Maclear, *op. cit.*
71. Doyle & Maitland, *op. cit.*
72. Maclear, *op. cit.*
73. Doyle & Maitland, *op. cit.*
74. Kattenberg, P., *The Vietnam Trauma in American Foreign Policy*, Transaction Books, 1979.
75. Fallows, J., *New York Times*, March 1982.
76. Maclear, *op. cit.*

Index

Figures in **bold** refer to illustrations

Agent Orange **32**, 33
air warfare 26–7
anti-war movement 21, 38, 40–41, 51
atrocities 20, 30–31, 35

Bao Dai 7, 10
"boat people" 45
bombing raids by United States 17, 18, 26, 38, 39
Britain 10, **41**, 50–51
Buddhists **34**

Calley, Lieutenant W.L. 30, **31**
Cambodia 4, 6, 38, 50
casualties 5
   American 5, 19, 20, 25, 40, **49**
   French 4, 12
   Vietnamese 4, 5, 18, 20, 25, 44
censorship of news 46–7
chemical warfare 32–3
China 10, 11, 12, 16
   aid to North Vietnam 36, 37
Cochin-China 5, 6, 11
communism 4, 9, 11
   takeover of South Vietnam 43
   world threat 15, 24
   see also Indochina Communist Party, Vietcong
CORDS plan 35
cost of the war 4

defoliation 32–3
Diem, Ngo Dinh 14–15, 52
Dien Bien Phu, battle of 13
Domino Theory 15
drugs 24, 34, 45

economic aid to North Vietnam 36, 37
   to South Vietnam 35
economic development 44–5

France 4, 6–7, 10–13

Giap, Vo Nguyen 12–13, 52
guerrilla warfare 5, 22–3, 48

helicopters in warfare 28–9
Ho Chi Minh 8–11, 14, 18, 54
Ho Chi Minh City 45
Ho Chi Minh Trail 14, 19, 26, 33, 36, 38

Indochina 5, 6
   see also Laos; Cambodia; Cochin-China
Indochina Communist Party 8–9
Indochinese War 10–13

Japan 4, 9
Johnson, Lyndon B. 16–17, 21, 48, 53

Kennedy, John F. 15, 32, 48, 53
Kent State University, Ohio 40
Khmer Rouge 50

Laos 4, 6, 15, 38

McCarthy, Eugene 41
media **16**, **18**, **20**, **21**, 46, **51**
morale of troops 24–5

napalm **32**
National Front for the Liberation of Vietnam 14
National Liberation Front for South Vietnam 15
Nixon, Richard M. 37, 38–9, 54
North Vietnam 4, 13, 14, 16–17, 18, 36–7
   military strategy 15, 20–25, 26
   control of media 47
   takes over Saigon 42–3
   women fighters **26**, 36, **37**

Operation Flaming Dart 16–17
Operation Phoenix 35
Operation Ranch Hand 32
Operation Rolling Thunder 17
orphans 44

Pathet Lao 15
Phnom Penh **50**
propaganda **17**, **27**, **35**, **36**, **39**, **41**, **46**, 47
public opinion (U.S.) 21, 32, 38, **39**, 40–41, 42, 46–7, 51

refugees **12**, 45
Rusk, Dean 41, 46, 48

search and destroy missions 18–19, 23
South Vietnam 4, 13, 14, 18, 34–5, 42
   air force 26–7
   prisoners of North Vietnam 44
   taken over by North Vietnam 42–3
Soviet Union 4, 9, 11, 12, 16, 50

technology in warfare 26–9
television, impact on public opinion of 46
Tet Offensive 20–21, 40, 46
Thieu, Nguyen Van 18, 42, 43, 55
Truman, Harry S. 11, 55

United States 4, 11, 13, 15, 40–41, 48, 50
   atrocities 30–1
   casualties 5, 19, 20, 25, 40
   military strategy 17, 23, 28–9, 32–3, 38, 48–9
   morale of troops 24–5, 31
   public opinion 21, 38, 40–41, 46–7
   troop levels 15, 17, 19, 22, 40

Vietcong 5, 14, 16, 18–19, 23, **24**, **30**, 35
   atrocities 20, **21**, 30–31
Vietminh 9, 13
Vietnam
   nationalism 7
   reconstruction 44–5
   under French rule 6–7
Vietnamization 38

war crimes 30–31
Westmoreland, William C. 18, 46, 48, 55
World War II 9, 10

Picture Acknowledgments

The author and publishers would like to thank the following for allowing their illustrations to be reproduced in this book: Centre for the Study of Cartoons and Caricature, University of Kent (V. Weisz, *Evening Standard*) 16, (N. Garland, *Daily Telegraph*) 47 (bottom); Embassy of the Socialist Republic of Vietnam 5, 17 (right), 24, 26, 27 (bottom), 35 (right), 37 (both), 39, 42, 45 (bottom); Mary Evans Picture Library 9; John Frost 15 (right), 21 (top), 31; Military Archive and Research Services (US Army) 4, 17 (left) and 35 (left); Peter Newark 6, 8, 27 (top), 29, 41 (bottom); Oxfam 50; Popperfoto 22, 25, 38, 41 (top), 52 (left), 53; The Research House 13, 28, (U.S. Navy) 43; Topham Picture Library *cover*, 10, 11, 12, 14, 18, 20, 21 (bottom), 23, 30, 32 (both), 33, 34, 36, 44, 45 (top), 47 (top), 48, 49 (both), 51, 52 (right), 54, 55; Wayland Picture Library 46. The maps on pages 7, 15 and 19 were supplied by Peter Bull Artwork Studio.